# My Football Hero: Jack Grealish

*Learn all about your favourite footballing star*

Rockmount Sports

## © Copyright 2022-All rights reserved.

The content contained within this book may not be reproduced, duplicated or transmitted without direct written permission from the author or the publisher.

Under no circumstances will any blame or legal responsibility be held against the publisher, or author, for any damages, reparation, or monetary loss due to the information contained within this book, either directly or indirectly.

Legal Notice:

This book is copyright protected. It is only for personal use. You cannot amend, distribute, sell, use, quote or paraphrase any part, or the content within this book, without the consent of the author or publisher.

Disclaimer Notice:

Please note the information contained within this document is for educational and entertainment purposes only. All effort has been executed to present accurate, up to date, reliable, complete information. No warranties of any kind are declared or implied. Readers acknowledge that the author is not engaged in the rendering of legal, financial, medical or professional advice. The content within this book has been derived from various sources. Please consult a licensed professional before attempting any techniques outlined in this book.

By reading this document, the reader agrees that under no circumstances is the author responsible for any losses, direct or indirect, that are incurred as a result of the use of the information contained within this document, including, but not limited to, errors, omissions, or inaccuracies.

# Table of Contents

Introduction: Jack Grealish—The Man

    Personal Stats:

Chapter 1: The Great Grealish Transfer

Chapter 2: Where It All Began

    Great-Great-Granddad: Football Legend!

    Birmingham to Solihull

    Good Catholic Schools

    Gaelic Football

    Passion for Football

    Scrappy Start at Highgate United

Chapter 3: Aston Villa, Jack's Dream

    Jim the Talent Spotter

    Aston Villa Academy

    Moving up Through the Ranks

    Give Us a chance!

    Never Forget Where You Came From

Chapter 4: Jack Grealish—Ireland International

    Irish Youth Teams

    Stalked by England

    Starting for Ireland Under-21

    Tough Choices: Play for Ireland or England?

Chapter 5: Lend Us Jack, Please!

    Jack at Notts County—Learning the Trade

    Jack's First Match at Notts

    Notts County's "Great Escape"

    Jack, Come Back!

Chapter 6: Back to Aston Villa

    Starting for the Claret and Blues

    Jack Signs Villa Deal

    Back to the Office

    The View From the Bench

    Aston Villa Fires Lambert

Chapter 7: Relegation Humiliation

    The Parade of the Clowns Managers

    Breaking Bad Records

    Never Forget Where You Came From

    Falling Off the Bottom of the League

    Sold off Cheap by the Americans

Chapter 8: Captain Jack

    Fighting in the Championship

    Jack Gets Knocked Back

    So, So, So Close

    Fractured Jack

    Jack Grealish Gets the Armband

    Learning to Lead

Chapter 9: Promotion: Getting Up and Hanging On

    Up the Down Ladder: Playoff Semi-Finals

    His Royal Highness the Worried Fan

Chapter 10: Jack Grealish—Villa's Houdini

    Tax Man: "Pay up or Go Out of Business!"

    Villans Fight On: UP THE VILLA!

    Empty Stands!

    Jack Grealish: Escape Artist

    Going up Further!

    Diving Diva or Foul Magnet?

    Bad Boy Jack

Chapter 11: England's Fan Favorite

    Jack's Early English Career

    UEFA Euro 2020 (2021)

    Super, Super-Sub Jack

    Reaching Out for Euro Glory

    One Hand On the Cup

    Penalty Drama at UEFA Euro Final

    What Next?

Honors

Some Jack Grealish Trivia

Great Grealish Moments

References

# Introduction:

# Jack Grealish—The Man

# Personal Stats:

- Date of Birth
    - ☐ 10 September 1995
- Place of Birth
    - ☐ Birmingham
- Height
    - ☐ 1.75m/5ft. 9in.
- Weight
    - ☐ 70kg/154lb/11st.
- Preferred foot
    - ☐ right
- Nationality
    - ☐ Republic of Ireland and England
- Clubs played for
    - ☐ Notts County; Aston Villa; Manchester City
- Supports
    - ☐ Aston Villa
- Position
    - ☐ left winger/attacking midfielder
- Jersey Numbers
    - ☐ #10 for Aston Villa; #10 for Manchester City; #7 for England

# Chapter 1: The Great Grealish Transfer

No English club ever paid more money for a player than Manchester City. They had to pay £100, 000, 000 to tear him away from Aston Villa. A hundred million pounds! Aston Villa fans are still heartbroken, but the Manchester City machine knows what it's doing. Jack Grealish is worth every penny.

The Sky Blue scouts were looking for an attacker. They needed to strengthen their midfield. City's defensive line was armour-plated. Astonishingly, they only let in 32 goals in the 2020-2021 Premier League season. On the other end though, they only scored 83 goals. This was down from 102 the season before. They needed more attacking firepower if they wanted to stay on top. It was easy to put Grealish at the top of their wish list! They started to see if they could get him.

Jack Grealish has a frightening skill-set on the ball. He has impressive Premier League stats. He scored eight goals and put through five assists in 2019-2020 for Villa. That sounds good. It is good! But he was off and injured for 15 games! In 2020-2021 he scored 6 goals and gave 10 assists in only 26 appearances. He wore the number 7 shirt for England under-21s in Toulon in 2016. He scored 3 goals over 6 games. In the 2013-2014 season, he went out as a youth loan to Notts

County. They wanted to keep him. Aston Villa wanted him back badly, though. Things were going disastrously for Villa. Even with Jack back in the team, they got relegated in 2016. In 2019 Jack Grealish became captain. Aston Villa then fought its way back up into the Premier League. He was not an all-out striker, but he lit up the midfield. It's easy to understand how a footballing chess player, like manager Pep Guardiola, would have his eye on the man.

We don't know what happened behind the scenes. Buyouts and transfers happen in boardrooms, not on football fields. Agents for the clubs and the player met together to fight over him. We do know that Villa was offering Grealish a contract paying out £200, 000 a week for him to stay. In the spring of 2021, the newspapers rumoured that Jack was leaving Villa. Headlines claimed Manchester City was trying to buy out Grealish. It was a nasty shock to the Villa fans! But no Claret and Blue fan was surprised that they had to pay so much for him.

Grealish wore numbers 7, 8, 10, 11, 12, 15, and 16 for the Villa under-21s. Then he wore 40 for a while for the Aston Villa squad. In the end, he settled on number 10. If he wanted to wear number 10, no one was going to object! Nobody has been more impressive at Aston Villa over the last ten years. He scored 17 goals with 20 assists in the big silverware competitions. When Aston

Villa dropped down to the Championship they bounced right back when Jack became captain.

He did not find it easy to move on. "It was obviously a difficult few months," he wrote on Twitter, "because I have been an Aston Villa fan for my whole life." (Skysports, 2021) He wrote this heartbroken letter to his fans:

*"I've been at Aston Villa for 19 years and I've been a fan my whole life. I've come up through the ranks and captained my club back to the top tier of English football. It's impossible to put my feelings into words, but I'll try.*

*When I first came to Villa I had my own personal dreams and ambitions like getting into the first team, scoring my first goal & scoring the winner in a derby. It wasn't until we got relegated that I felt a greater sense of purpose.*

*Every time I put on the Villa shirt I played with my heart on my sleeve. Being given the armband was both a privilege and an honor for me and my family and I've loved every minute of it.*

*I want to thank the manager and my teammates, I'll never forget everything we achieved together... and to the fans who have supported me through everything, I can't thank you enough.*

*To all my coaches and all the people who work at the club behind the scenes who have done so much for me over the years-thank you.*

*I'll always be a Villa fan — I love this club with all my heart and I hope you understand my reasons for seeking a new challenge.*

*The club are in great hands, the manager, the lads, the new signings coming in — it's an exciting time to be a Villa fan. I'll see you all again soon. Until next time. UP THE VILLA. Jack."* (Lynch, 2021)

Jack Grealish took over the number 10 jersey when he went over to Manchester City. He is now doing exactly what his new team hoped for. He puts through two or three passes to open players in every game he plays. Jack Grealish intimidates defences, and ties up defenders. You can't give him an inch, but he'll take it off you anyway.

This is the story of how a Birmingham boy became the footballing genius that the top teams fight for—or fear!

# Chapter 2: Where It All Began

## Great-Great-Granddad: Football Legend!

Jack has claret in his blood. He grew up in an Aston Villa home in an Aston Villa dynasty. There was a set of black and white photos of his great-great-grandfather on the wall of his family home. Old Billy Garraty played for England back in the early 1900s. He was also part of Aston Villa's FA Cup-winning team in 1910. Jack Grealish's pride in Aston Villa went back a long way.

His dad had been to matches with Jack's granddad. His Granddad had been to matches with his great-grandad. His great-grandfather had been to watch his great-great-grandfather play for Villa! Jack Grealish has always held a season ticket for Villa Park, the home of the Claret and Blues since 1897. Their family never missed a match.

If he stood on a chair, Jack could get a closer look at his great-great-grandfather. Billy Garraty as a young man had an impressive gull-wing mustache. Aston Villa's strip in those days was a weird hand-knitted jersey and knee-length shorts that hung from the waist. The boots were crazy—how could you kick a ball with boots that had big round toe-caps? The ball though—that took the cake! A massive, baggy-looking brown thing, hand-stitched out of eight leather panels. Could it even roll?

Jack's school football kit was technologically way more advanced than Billy Garraty's kit had been.

Jack also inherited talent. Garraty is still Villa's 8th highest goal scorer (111). In the 1899-1900 season he won the golden-boot: 27 goals in 33 matches! I wonder what the old man would make of his high octane great-great-grandson?

Jack Grealish started his international career playing for Republic of Ireland youth teams. He had the right to play for either England or Ireland. The Grealishes had strong Irish roots in Dublin, Galway, and Kerry. The Grealish kids, though, had grown up in Solihull. They felt quite torn between their Midlands surroundings and their Irish roots. They had an Irish name, went to a Roman Catholic Church, and attended Roman Catholic schools. All very Irish. But they grew up in the industrial heart of England.

Jack had to work out who he was. It is not so simple to forge your own identity when you have to choose between two cultures.

Many kids find themselves in exactly the same position as Jack Grealish.

# Birmingham to Solihull

Grealish was born in Birmingham, but the family soon migrated to Solihull. Jack's parents liked having children and loved their kids. There were five children altogether: Kevan (born in 1994). Then Jack (1995). Then Keelan (1999), who sadly died as a baby. Then came Kiera (2002). And Hollie last of all (2004). They filled their house to overflowing. Jack grew up with fighting and friendship. His brother and sisters knocked the corners off him. Jack thrived on competition from the get-go!

Hollie had a momentary break in oxygen to her brain as she was being born. She was unlucky enough to get cerebral palsy. She has spent too much time in hospital, and her siblings support her to the maximum. She supports them right back. Jack reckons she inspires him with her courage and cheerfulness. It seems that the Grealish kids are all fighters.

Jack's dad, Kevin, is a skilled plasterer. He accepts, though, that his son will not follow in his footsteps. Kevin and Jack's mum, Karen, realized from very early on that Jack would have a different trade. They have no complaints. Kevin's steady income was enough to keep and educate the kids. Sadly, though, one of the five Grealish kids never made it out of infancy.

# Good Catholic Schools

For many of us, school is the thing you have to do so you can play sports. That's the way Jack saw it! He went to Our Lady of Compassion Roman Catholic Primary School. Jack learned the basics there. He also graduated with thousands of hours of playground football! The school produced good teams.

The grade 6 team noticed Jack's amazing ability to control the ball. They drafted him while he was still in grade 4. With Jack Grealish the team won the U12 Birmingham Schools Cup. Already at that age he could read the game and put the ball into places nobody thought he could go. Two years later, Jack and his team were joint-winners of the Solihull Schools Cup final.

St Anne's and Four Oaks turn out better readers and mathematicians. But Our Lady turns out the footballers!

Jack went on to St. Peter's Roman Catholic Secondary School. His team coach there, Tom Seickell, is not surprised at Jack's success. Seickell remembers how often Jack used to get kicked and tripped and shoved—but he bounced up every time! He was incredibly quick and decisive, and usually got tackled after he had got the ball through! Jack finished school in grade 10. His team made it to the final of the Birmingham Schools Cup final, played at Villa Park.

He was going to get to know Bodymoor Heath really well!

## Gaelic Football

Jack Grealish's dad reckons that Gaelic football toughened Jack. He would have done well at whatever sport he chose. For a long time, he looked set to be a Gaelic footballer.

Gaelic football works like this: the objective is to score one point by getting the ball over the crossbar. Or you score three points by getting the ball in the net. You can carry the ball for four steps. Then you either have to drop it on your foot and catch it again, or you must pass it. To get the ball off your opposition, you can just grab it. Or else you can sideswipe your opponent with a shoulder charge. Watch a match on Youtube to decide whether you are going to try out for a local club!

Jack never stopped playing football. From the age of 10 to 14, Jack Grealish was playing two sports. His Gaelic Football club was John Mitchel's Hurling and Camogie Club of Warwickshire GAA. Jack always took sports seriously! He scored a point for the GAA team once! Eventually, however, he had to choose to leave Gaelic football behind. His football fans are happy with that!

Every experience in life leaves its mark, and all training gives you skills. Jack is only in the lightweight boxing weight range. He gets constantly roughed up by defences. When you tackle Jack Grealish, though, you tackle a Gaelic footballer. That won't always end up well for you!

## Passion for Football

Paul Merson was Jack's hero. Merson was an Aston Villa attacking midfielder. He had 140 starts for the Claret and Blues (scoring 46 goals and giving 43 assists). He also won 21 caps for England (to go with his 4 under-21 England caps). Jack paid close attention to Merson's play. Jack eventually played in the same position for Villa and England. It says something about Jack's ambition, but also his footballing brain. He knew where his skill set could take him. So he studied at the best footballing university. He watched a skilled player doing the job he wanted, while constantly working at his own skills.

Jack always had raw talent, though. When he was a four-year-old playing in the local park, people were already amazed by his dribbling. He was easily able to run with his bigger brother and cousins. His dad noted this and made sure he got the chance to join a local club as soon as he could.

# Scrappy Start at Highgate United

Jack's dad got to know the coach of the Highgate United Football Club. One thing led to another, and Jack's dad took him along to try out for the Youth Program at Highgate. He impressed everyone. In 2001 he joined the under-8 squad.

Jack's dad was always looking out for ways to support his son. Grealish says his dad took him to every match. He still goes to watch every match Jack plays in. His mum comes whenever she can, too. Jack's parents completely backed him to succeed. Kevin Grealish is a "celebrity parent." He deserves his fame. He played an essential role in Jack getting to where he is.

Who wouldn't want this little terrier of a footballer in their team! Highgate gave little Jack Grealish his first taste of team football with the under-8s at The Coppice in Tythe Barn Lane. That nearly got cut short. Highgate United was extremely hard up for cash that season. They were going to have to shut down the youth division. There was no money for a team strip. The parents mobilized to find sponsors to keep their kids playing.

One of the club parents asked a local "pre-owned" car dealer, Martin Smallbone, for a £200 sponsorship. Smallbone cheerfully kitted them out in orange jerseys. So "Smallbone Car Sales" was Jack Grealish's first sponsorship! Smallbone reckons it never helped him sell a car, but he is happy to have been part of Jack's success story. Who knows? That bright orange jersey might have helped to draw the attention of Jim Thomas.

Who pays attention to a six-year-old kid playing football? Jim Thomas.

# Chapter 3: Aston Villa, Jack's Dream

"There's this old bloke watching the kids play football!" Actually, it's not as creepy as it sounds. This old bloke was one of a kind. He was a specialist talent scout for Aston Villa, and he knew what talent looks like in a six-year-old.

## Jim the Talent Spotter

Jim Thomas has a string of successes to boast about.

He spotted Andre Green playing for Castle Bromwich under-9s. He spotted Eesah Suliman over at Moseley. Jack Clarke caught his eye at Arden Forest. Callum O'Hare is another one of his picks. Jim spotted Jack Grealish at the age of six, playing for the under-8s of Highgate United. Jack impressed him by dribbling through the whole team. He had a low center of gravity and explosive speed. Control of the ball was already his trademark skill.

Jim Thomas talked with Jack's parents. He described the specialized training at Bodymoor Heath, Aston

Villa's training ground. Jim liked to get talented young players into proper training before they were 10.

Once you got into Aston Villa Academy you would never be the same.

## Aston Villa Academy

The Villa Academy is the Hogwarts of the footballing world.

The Academy works with players from under-8 to under-19. Jack Grealish joined in 2001, in the early days of the Academy. The Academy aims to develop more than just footballing skills. It aims to prepare players for professional footballing life. Villa invests in lifestyle and health issues as much as coaching. Young, talented footballers often miss out on schooling opportunities. The Academy tries to make sure they know enough to make sensible life choices.

Compare this curriculum to what they teach at school.

Outfield players get to hone the *technical* skills they have. They study and practice passing through tight channels and two-touch passing. They go through exercises to improve receiving the ball. They learn dribbling in various scenarios. They get shooting under pressure practice and practice in keeping ball possession. There is training in manipulating the ball across your body and turning away out of pressure.

Outfield players also get to learn or develop *tactical* play. They have to understand how to play out from the back. They get trained how to play the ball through defences. They get taught how to play out of a situation where there is an extra man covering them. They have to learn the strategies of central attack and attack out wide. Counterattack options need to be studied and practiced. Defending as an individual or in a group needs to become second nature. Hunting and retrieving ball possession is also a skill that needs sharpening into an instinct.

Goalkeepers have their own unique syllabus. They study the various passes needed to support players. They learn to read the best options for ball distribution. The goalkeeper has to work on trained instinct. Goalies need to train for one-on-one attacks, early shots, and how to choose the best position for the cross. They need to be the best organizers and communicators on the pitch (Aston Villa FC Academy, 2021).

That's a taste of what goes on. There is much more. Kevin Grealish knows that there is a right way and a wrong way to plaster a wall. His son, Jack, knows that there is a right and a wrong way to play football. He looks like he operates entirely on flair. He certainly does have flair. He is also highly trained.

# Moving up Through the Ranks

The only way was up! It was deeply satisfying to train in a system that took football so seriously. The more seriously you take something, the more fun it is. The best talent in the Midlands was there to push Jack at Bodymoor Heath. At the same time, he was helping his team earn glory at school. Jim Thomas had picked a "really good 'un'" this time!

Bryan Jones was Jack's Director at the Academy throughout his career. He remembers Jack always worked incredibly hard. He also had a brilliantly positive attitude. Jack knew he had talent—at 14' he was still punching above his weight, playing with the 16-year-olds. He never thought that he was better than he *was*, though. He was always measuring himself against the strongest opposition he could find. Jack was curious about what he could do, not arrogant about how much others admired him.

By 2012, Grealish was considered good enough to be chosen as a substitute. He was on the bench for a Premier League home match against Chelsea. He was never used, so he sat there feeling helpless as Chelsea crushed Villa 4-2. Villa lost the plot. Jack Grealish could do nothing except smolder in the stands.

His career with the under-19s was on a hot streak, though. In the 2012-2013 season, Aston Villa's under-19 team was an overwhelming force. They won the

NextGen series. Jack Grealish was a key player in that triumph.

The best 24 under-19 teams from across Europe played in the NextGen tournament. Aston Villa was second to Sporting CP in their stage 1 group. They lost 1-3 to Sporting CP, and 0-1 to PSV Eindhoven. They drew 2-2 with Celtic. They beat Celtic (2-1), PSV Eindhoven (2-0), and Sporting CP in the second leg (a 5-1 thrashing). In the knockout rounds they beat Ajax 2-1 in the round of 16. They beat Olympiakos 1-0 in the quarters. They then beat Sporting CP 3-1 in the semis (Grealish scored in stoppage time). They capped off their fantastic run by taking the trophy against Chelsea with a 2-0 result.

Aston Villa Academy was producing top results, and Jack was happily in the center of it all.

## Give Us a chance!

The Academy was training up spectacularly talented footballers. The message, though, was not getting through to the management of the senior team. Aston Villa was not doing at all well in the Premier League. Lots of fans blamed this on them ignoring their own home-grown talent! What is the use of training these guys if you're not going to play them?

Grealish was knocking on a difficult door.

Paul Lambert was struggling as manager of the Claret and Blues. The Villans were losing more than they were winning (with a win-draw-loss ratio of 34-26-35). Lambert never got on with the young Jack Grealish, though. Grealish complained on Twitter that Academy players weren't getting many opportunities to play for the senior side. It was true, but it did not please Lambert! In fact, it stalled Jack's career for a while. Managers have a lot of power. Jack had not yet learned the tactical value of keeping your mouth shut!

Lambert followed a cautious path with young talent. He thought that Grealish ("the kid" as he called him) hadn't developed a big match temperament yet. Instead, Lambert used less talented but more "experienced" sign-ins from outside. He did not trust the very source of talent that the Academy had been set up for. Jack was not the only player who got caught up in the under-21 Villa bottleneck.

Jack returned from Notts County. Lambert reluctantly brought Grealish on as a substitute. It was in a Premier League clash with Manchester City on 7 May 2014. Aston Villa only had 27% of possession as the sky blue boa constrictor crushed the life out of them. Coming on with the team 2-0 down in the 88th minute Grealish did not exactly have scope for his talent. He did give Fabian Delph an assist by putting the ball on Delph's left foot. Delph's shot was blocked. Manchester City scored another two goals. Final score: 4-0. It was where Jack wanted to be, but it was a forgettable day.

# Never Forget Where You Came From

Although he always was a Villa fan, Jack has never forgotten that he owed his start to Highgate United. It's one of his best qualities. He is grateful to the people who have helped him. He has even joined his mates from his days at Highgate United in a Butlins Football Tournament. How cool is that! To have Jack Grealish on your side at Butlins! I bet Highgate's opponents would not have been pleased. Jack doesn't forget people just because he's become a superstar. We see this happening over and over.

# Chapter 4: Jack Grealish—Ireland International

He never forgot that he was Irish. His spirit of "never forgetting where he came from" brought him into the Irish National setup.

His early play at the national level was all for Ireland. Villa manager Lambert might have had his doubts about Jack Grealish. The Republic of Ireland, on the other hand, had every confidence in him.

## Irish Youth Teams

Jack was eligible to play for either Ireland or England. He had Irish ancestry, but he had also been born in England. The need to choose one or the other worried him. Grealish played for youth teams of Ireland from 2011 to 2014. It was not a simple life off the field. He rose to the occasion though, and became one of Ireland's most popular players.

Jack was getting relatively little playing time at Aston Villa. The English selectors had nothing to see. In a way that drove him to Ireland. There was confusion between Academy management and First Team management at Villa. This had the spin-off result of pushing their younger stars to look elsewhere. Jack would never willingly leave his beloved Aston Villa, of course. He needed stronger opponents, though. Playing national age level football for the Republic of Ireland gave him exactly what he needed.

He was 14 on his first outing for Ireland in 2010. He played for their under-15 team. Jordan Graham was another of Villa's Academy players who made that team. Ireland dished out a 5-0 hammering to Northern Ireland. Grealish sent in two pinpoint corners that Kyle McFadden and Gary O'Neill netted. Sam Byrne also headed in a perfect cross from Grealish. Jack was making his mark, alongside other future stars.

In 2011, Jack was in the mix for two under-17 internationals. He was in the team for a match against Serbia, played at Ferrycarrig Park, Wexford. It ended all square at 1-1. After that came the qualifying rounds for the UEFA championships. The Republic of Ireland faced the Czech Republic, Kazakhstan, and Liechtenstein in group 4. Grealish scored one in an 8-0 smear of Liechtenstein, and another in a 1-1 draw against Kazakhstan. They went down 0-1 to the Czech Republic. They advanced to the next round by coming second in their group.

The elite round was a disaster for the Republic of Ireland, though. They lost all three matches against Netherlands, Serbia, and Albania. Jack's reputation did not suffer. He scored a goal in a losing cause against Albania. That made three goals for the tournament. Not bad for a midfielder. Grealish had become a midfield attacker of note. It came at a cost, though. The more his fame grew, the more people wanted to grab him for their teams.

## Stalked by England

England actively hunted Grealish. Ireland fought to keep him. Aston Villa beat off high price offers for a transfer. Jack was the football in the boardroom competition. He did not like it. He has never been happy at playing politics. When you are so good, though, you attract politics wherever you go. The England establishment had already inked him in for their 2011 under-seventeen squad. Jack was only 15 at the time and had to decide whether to make the move. He decided not to.

Everybody knew what England was doing, and once again Jack's career hit a roadblock. Ireland didn't want to train him up for England. They left him out for three October qualifiers for UEFA Under-21s in 2013. He also got left out of an Irish friendly against Denmark. The Irish manager, though, was still trying to convince Jack to stay. He talked with Jack and his parents and promised him a solid future for Ireland. That settled the debate for a while. But England never stopped trying, and Jack was not convinced.

Jack knew that everybody wanted a piece of him.

He freaked out when England and Ireland both called him up to play for Under-17 National teams, at the same time! He set out traveling with the English team. He was under such stress, though, that one day he collapsed. He woke up on the bathroom floor. That got him sent home. This was a good thing at the time because it meant that he was able to attend trials in Ireland with a clear mind. Of course, he aced the trialing in Ireland, and he could just focus on his football for the next few years. As he tells it, he loved every moment of playing for the Boys in Green.

## Starting for Ireland Under-21

In 2014 Jack was Ireland's under-21 player of the year.

He had cracked the under-21s the year before when he came on as a sub against the Faroe Islands. That was the Robbie Keene show, who scored all the goals in the match. Ireland comfortably defeated the Faroe Islands 3-0. But it was a milestone for Jack Grealish. Playing for the under-21s put him within range of Irish Senior football. Everything was not right, though. Jack was struggling.

In 2014 there were rumors that Grealish would not make himself available for the Republic of Ireland. He did. He was in the team that went down 2-0 against

Germany in August that year. There were constant signs that he was taking strain. The off-field pressure never eased up. Ireland. England. Villa. Jack had to make choices.

## Tough Choices: Play for Ireland or England?

The Irish senior team offered him a spot. Jack said no. In October 2014 he turned down a place in the Under-21 game against Norway. He chose instead to play for Villa in a friendly. The newspapers were full of headlines: "Grealish was going to play for the Ireland Senior team." False. "Grealish was the Under-21 man of the year." True. "Grealish was taking a break from Internationals." True. "Grealish had been called up again for the Irish seniors." True. "He was going to play." False.

Jack was exhausted. Both Ireland and England were hounding him. Life was getting way too complicated. Things had been tough in England too. He decided instead to focus on his childhood dream of playing for the Claret and Blues. In all the uncertainty of his international options, Villa was easy to put first. He had always put his club first. It was the simple choice.

There were complications. Lambert, the manager, distrusted him. The club was at the bottom of the league . Jack had to decide whether it was good for his career to be on a sinking ship.

Jack didn't abandon old friends. He chose to focus on Aston Villa.

# Chapter 5: Lend Us Jack, Please!

Would you loan Jack Grealish to another team?

The four months Jack Grealish spent at Notts County changed his life. Strong clubs loan out their young players who show talent. It gives the players real-life experience as professionals. It lets clubs see if they can handle pressure. And it gives everybody a change of perspective.

League One teams get top-quality young professionals for cheap. Jack Grealish was an amazing bargain!

## Jack at Notts County—Learning the Trade

In 2013, Villa was doing badly, and so was Notts County. Jack Grealish, of course, never imagined *leaving* the Villans. He was on loan to learn. His job was to apply all his mind to the problems of his temporary new team. He made 39 appearances, and scored 5 goals.

One of the big lessons on offer was how to play for a struggling team. Jack's solution was simple. Make it a winning team!

Notts County was really in trouble, though. They were facing relegation, at the bottom of League One, England's third division. Their Boss, Shaun Derry, was a desperate man. He was also shrewder than Lambert at Villa. Derry appreciated the spectacular record of Jack Grealish. Borrowing this player was a no-brainer.

17-year-old Grealish turned out for 37 of the 46 League matches. Notts County's job was to teach Jack how to be a professional footballer. They desperately needed him as a player, too.

## Jack's First Match at Notts

Jack played with 7 on his shirt at Notts, on the right wing—not the position we are used to seeing him. Everything was education, though. He thrived in the midfield, wherever he found himself. That's where they put him, but he didn't stay there. You never knew where he would pop up on the field!

The day after he signed with Notts, he was out there fighting for his team. Notts were struggling in a game against Milton Keynes. They threw him on as a sub in the 59th minute. He was put in at left-wing, actually, but he had a fairly ordinary start. Notts County lost 3-

1, and it seemed like they were doomed to drop to League Two. This was their fourth year in League One, but they were at the very bottom of the table.

The more he played, the more Jack found his groove. As he warmed up to his work, the future of Notts seemed to change. Jack's first professional goal came for Notts in a match against Gillingham. It was played at Meadow Lane on 7 December 2013. It was a bit of classic Grealish magic. He collects the clearance just outside the left-hand side of the box (as he's playing). Then he runs right across the entire defence. He beats four challenges. He draws the goalie and then smashes it off the right foot past the goalie into the top of the net. The Notts fans go crazy!

He didn't wait long to score his second goal either. The next weekend he was first on the list of the scorers as Notts County annihilated Colchester City 4-0. Grealish was assured of his place in the team.

## Notts County's "Great Escape"

Jack would never say he did it all by himself.

The Boss had put together as strong an outfit as he could. He did not have much to work with. It did have key players like Alan Sheehan and Ronan Murray. The loan players needed to hit the ground running, all 14 of them. Notts had loan players every year. Some were better than others. That year there was Jack. Another one of them was a young Callum McGregor. With the help of his midfield mates, McGregor scored 12 goals that season! Josh Vela was another one. Callum Ball was signed on loan from Derby County. The young guns had a lot to prove. They wanted to impress their home clubs. They also wanted to win games! This year manager Shaun Derry had got some fighting combinations! Having so many changes, though, does not help a team to gel.

It was not an easy season, even with the skills and hard work of the young loan players. Notts County was in trouble. Two years before, they finished third in the league. In 2013 they looked like they were sunk. They were up and down. They beat both Crewe Alexandra and Colchester United 4-0. On the other hand, they played some really bad games, too. The low point came in a 0-6 defeat to Rotherham United. One to forget.

It didn't look like Notts County's 125th year in the league was going to end well. They bobbed along on the relegation line the entire season. They developed a reputation of being "easy to beat". Jack Grealish and his mates had other ideas.

It was a fight to the finish. If you ended the season in 20th place you were safe from relegation. At place 20 you keep your sponsorships and you keep your players. You can build up to a better place next season. Relegation games pitch your exhausted team against the top teams of the lower league. The young lions of the lower league are hungry to make their own way up in the world.

It was too close to call. Their last six matches had their fans chewing their nails.

Game 40 Notts won against Colchester (2-0). Grealish came on as a late substitution. They were safely up to 19th place.

Game 41 they lost 3-1 against Brentford. They dropped to place 23!

Game 42 they won against Port Vale (4-2), with Grealish menacing on the left wing. Back up to the new prize line of being number 20.

Game 43 they lost against Bristol City (2-1). With only three more games to play, they were down to 22. Ring the alarm bells!

Their win in game 44 against Crawley Town came with a single goal to nothing. It only brought them up one place to 21—still too little. Grealish made a huge nuisance of himself on the left without much success, but one goal was enough to bring them up further.

They then got another win against Swindon Town (2-0). Sheehan picked up a beautiful through-ball from Grealish! That sealed Swindon Town's coffin. Victory in game 45 got them clear to place 19. They were not safe, though. If they lost their last game, they were going down.

Game 46 was an away game against Oldham Athletic. Notts had only won 3 out of 17 away games that season. If they lost they were out! It was a tense match, with both goals coming in the second half. Notts could not make their one-man advantage work for them. They scrambled a 1-1 draw! Notts County finished in 20th position! They celebrated as if they had won the silverware!

Notts County fans reckon it was Jack Grealish who inspired the season's unlikely result. They still miss him. Notts captain, Allan Sheehan, remembers his blistering pace on the ball. He also remembers that the 18-year-old Jack Grealish was "always confident but never arrogant." (Curtis, 2021) You don't have to boast if you really are the best. That year forged a bond between the two players. To this day Sheehan and Grealish still exchange messages on Twitter.

If Jack Grealish went to Notts County to get experience, he got exactly what he needed. He would be facing the same relegation difficulties back at the Claret and Blue. He had learned what the struggle to stay up was like!

## Jack, Come Back!

Manager Lambert still wasn't getting the best out of his Villa players. The club was still struggling in 2013/14.

Manchester City won the Premier League trophy that year by two small points off Liverpool. Aston Villa, down at the other end, finished at 15. Only three places above relegation! Aston Villa is one of the powerhouses of English football. They were not playing that way. The fans were getting impatient.

Lambert still did not trust Jack Grealish. He saw him working miracles at Notts County, though, so he wanted him back. The 2014-2015 season looked like it was going to be tough. All the clubs across the country were thinking about their squads. At Villa, Lambert had to make decisions about the club's rising Academy talent.

Jack came back at the worst time for the club. But he was going to turn it around.

# Chapter 6: Back to Aston Villa

Lambert was eventually forced to try Grealish. His other options were going nowhere.

## Starting for the Claret and Blues

Jack played for Aston Villa senior team at last! This was his dream, ever since he watched as a four-year-old with his dad and brother. It was the first time in more than 100 years that a family member had worn a Villa player's strip. The last one was his great-great-great-granddad, Billy Garraty. This was not the wooly jumper with the long blue sleeves and one-color socks of that ancient kit. But it was still Claret and Blue. Jack Grealish felt a twinge of awe and excitement as he pulled it on. Macron was their main sponsor that year. It was the most high-tech sports-wear product so far. It was 92% polyester, and 8% elastane, with breathable mesh inserts. This made it an efficient, tight fit. It wicked off sweat and was ideal for any weather.

Jack knew about the 1981-1982 season. That was the year Villa had won the European Cup. He knew all the club history. He knew Villa had won the silverware seven times in Football League First Division. He knew they had been FA Cup Champions five times. And they were the only club to win the UEFA Cup. He was itching to make his mark.

He wasn't on the field yet, though. Jack had been on the subs bench before. He knew the disappointment of being all kitted out but never used. This time it was a good game to miss. Aston Villa was showing their lack of class under Lambert, and the fans were leaving early. Lambert was sometimes bringing all 11 players back into defence. This was not a strategy to make the best use of Jack's talents. He got sent on, anyway. It was the 88th minute, with Villa down 2-0. In the final 6 minutes of play, Jovetic and Toure for City made it a 4-0 savaging. Jack only did a little scrambling defence. It was not his day.

Except it was his day. Nobody could take the Aston Villa Jersey away from him. Jack Grealish had played for his club.

## Jack Signs Villa Deal

Once a team starts to head down, it often keeps going. Grealish has always been cheerful. The smile gets a little tense, though, as the bad results start to flow. Jack was on another sinking ship. He had hopped back on just as it started to leak badly. Villa ended the 2013-2014 Premier League season down at 17. Lambert's strange defensive strategy of hiring "experienced" players did not work. The team that year was sluggish and easy to beat. Footballers like to win. Attackers like to attack. The dressing room was angry and embarrassed. The fans were seriously upset.

The stats make grim reading. At one stage Villa went for a five-match streak of not scoring a single goal! They didn't score any goals at all in the entire League Cup! They were still getting 30-40, 000 fans at Villa Park. The fans were not pleased!

Jack Grealish spent a lot of time glaring at the game from the substitutes' bench that season. He only played 17 times in 2014-2015, ten times as a substitute. Technically, he was now an Aston Villa player. He felt like he was being kept on the sidelines and was being kept on the sidelines.

Grealish was never going to sit still for long. In May of 2014, he played in the Hong Kong 7's Tournament. He does very well in this format. The intensity of the play in a fast, smaller playing area is perfect for his skill set. It gave him something to take his mind off his struggles with choosing national sides. It also distracted him from his frustrations with the Villa management. Unsurprisingly, Grealish came out as the top scorer with six goals.

## Back to the Office

It was a lot of fun. Then it was back to the office at Villa Park.

The job of a professional footballer is to train and play. Training is deadly serious and highly technical. Jack will get patched up on Mondays from any scrapes or bumps. The team's medical team will consider any injury or niggle, and then OK him for a week's training. Monday is a very light work-out, as the body recovers from yesterday's 90-minute battle. On Tuesday he hits the gym for 4-6 hours. First, he does weights in the footballer's gym at Bodymoor Heath. After that it's HIIT. HIIT is short for "High-intensity interval training." It's savage. You do short bursts of maximum effort training. Then you have a very short recovery time. After that, you repeat the exercise at the same intensity. Then take another short rest. Do that until you cannot do another set. It's easy to see how that gets a player fit enough for top-flight football!

On Wednesday it's team practice on the Bodymoor Heath training grounds. Nobody is allowed to watch these practice sessions—they don't want any spies taking notes of tactics. Thursday is another gym day. Friday you have to rest. And Saturday is "light cardio"—cycling or swimming or light gym work. Then you are ready for match day on Sunday.

# The View From the Bench

There is a special friendship that builds up among the substitutes. They are good enough to play, but not good enough to start. The first pick players were not making a good job of it, though. It was frustrating.

Grealish's second outing for Villa came at the start of the new season in August 2014. He came on at 71 minutes and had a short 25 minute run in the opening match of the season against Stoke City. It was a low-intensity match, compared to the last time the two teams met. This time Villa came out on top, 1-0. It was a good-enough comeback after the 4-1 thrashing Stoke City had given Villa in the previous season. Villa seemed solid enough. It was, unknown to Jack, going to be a season with only 9 more wins. Villa's 20 losses and 8 draws left it vulnerable to the havoc of the 2015-2016 season.

At this point, Jack took a break from international football. Villa offered him a four-year contract in September. The board had a little chat with Lambert, the manager. Somebody wanted to make sure Grealish stayed with the team. They were able to see how important he was.

After signing, Jack eventually got his first start. It was an FA Cup third-round fixture against Blackpool on 14 October 2014. His dad, Kevin, had to sit in their usual seats in the Doug Ellis stand without Jack. His son was playing for his team! Villa eased to a 1-0 win. Jack played for most of the game before he was substituted at 75 minutes. Kevin Grealish must have been really proud.

Jack went on to make 17 appearances for the senior team, mostly off the bench. He also played 8 times for the Premier League 2 tournament, the so-called "Reserve League." It was a year of hard, hard graft. All he wanted to do was be a permanent player for Villa. The ten times he was "not in squad" made him nervous. Did Aston Villa have long-term plans for him? A contract does not protect a player from being sold off. It was a tense year.

## Aston Villa Fires Lambert

Lambert still refused to play Grealish. It was one of several poor decisions that marked his leadership.

Aston Villa was down at 18th place in the league. They had only come up with 22 points. They had lost or drawn their last 10 matches, and they had lost their last five matches in a row. It was time to dump Paul Lambert. He had a shabby record: 34 wins, 26 draws, and an agonizing 55 losses. Everybody was relieved when he was booted in February 2015. Scott Marshall and Andy Marshall took over. They were caretakers until Villa could get a more effective manager. (An interesting point is that these two coaches are not related at all!)

The Marshalls made better use of Jack. They put him in the starting lineup for a match against Queens Park

Rangers on 7 April 2015. It ended in a high-scoring draw (3-3). Benteke got all three for Villa. The fans liked Jack, though. A lot. He set up the first goal. He took the ball through on the left wing with one of his mazy runs, and then passed right into space for Benteke. In the 17th minute, it took a superman save from Green to stop Grealish from scoring. Green denied Grealish again in the 54th minute. Grealish sent over a pinpoint pass. It drifted across the QPR goalmouth, begging for someone to touch it in. Nobody got there. Benteke scored later to level things at 3-all. It was yet another draw. One point is better than none, but three is the best.

In the end, Villa only won 7 matches in the season. They lost 14. They drew 17! They were lucky to avoid relegation at place 17 in the league. Christian Benteke almost single-handedly kept them up with his 13 goals. Most fans agree that Lambert had been a bad choice as manager. This was not the Villa that Jack had dreamed of joining. But it was the Villa he got into.

The FA Cup gave Villans something to smile about, though. They played brilliantly until the last match. Aston Villa entered the competition in the third round, as Premier League teams do. Benteke got them the single goal that brought them victory over Blackpool. Gil and Weiman scored for Villa in their fourth-round defeat of Bournemouth.

At that point, Lambert got the sack. At first, the team seemed to ride the change in managers as far as the FA cup was concerned. They went on to win the fifth-round tie against Leicester City 2-1, with Villa goals coming from Bacuna and Sinclair. They kept on winning. Their sixth fixture was against their old Midlands rival, West Bromwich Albion. Jack Grealish had been playing solidly. He was brought on as a sub, but was sent off for a double yellow in stoppage time of that match. He dived. Well, every Villa fan thinks it was yet another foul on him. But the ref showed him yellow and red, and he had to go. He joined West Bromwich Albion's Claudio Yacob in the sin bin. Jack's lack of discipline did not cost the club anything, fortunately. It was a simple 2-0 victory for Aston Villa. Delph and Sinclair were the scorers.

Then came Liverpool, with all to play for. The winner would go through to the final at Wembley. Benteke and Delph's two goals beat Coutinho's single. Jack was deeply involved in bringing the ball through to the goal scorers. After going 1-0 down, the team rallied and came back to win. It was a great day at Wembley! The win took the Villa through to their first final since 2000.

The fans waited eagerly for the FA Cup Final day. At Wembley. Against Arsenal. A full house with 89,283 fans in full voice. Prince William was cheering them on.

It did not go well for Villa. The stats confirm the horror story. Villa had only two shots at goal. Two. Neither was on target. They had zero corners. Zilch. Nothing. The side that beat Liverpool so well the week before just did not turn up. Jack Grealish played the whole humiliating 94 minutes. But he only really got time on the ball for about 20 minutes after half-time. One reporter called Aston Villa a "sleepwalking side" (Callow, 2015).

On the whole Aston Villa had survived the season. Under Tim Sherwood's management, they had avoided relegation. They *had* reached the FA Cup final. Sherwood made good use of Grealish in the midfield. Jack and his mates had a long road ahead of them, though. The 2015-2016 season turned out to be worse than they could imagine.

# Chapter 7: Relegation Humiliation

Villa had had a team in the top tier of English football since 1992. That was when the Premier League started. They have not yet won it, but they have always been in with a shout. They have ended the season in 6th place four times. Now they had spent two years only just squeaking through. The fans were expecting something much better from the Villans in 2016.

## The Parade of the Clowns Managers

In Africa they say that "A fish rots from its head downwards." Aston Villa was having rotten head problems. The managers were entering through a revolving door, as they say. O'Leary and O'Neill had lasted three or four years each. After that it was carnage. Houlier and McLeish each only lasted a year. Then came Lambert's disastrous three years. After that, the managers crumbled like the team.

Tim Sherwood lasted from February to October 2015. Rémi Garde only lasted the rest of that season. Roberto di Matteo held the post for a few months from June to October 2016. Steve Bruce seemed to steady the ship in his two years as Boss. Then Dean Smith led the club back into the Premier League.

The Boss is very important. He can make the side or destroy it. He sets the direction and the coaches train the players to play out the Boss' vision. Then the players are supposed to put the plan into action and win.

Villa had too many changing visions. The players were discouraged and confused. Even the most brilliant talent can't cope with that. Villa had its worst season ever. Kevin Grealish, Jack's dad, and all the Villa fans sat with their heads in their hands in the stands. The singing went quiet and spectators slipped away before the final whistle. Nobody likes to remember that desperate and discouraging season.

Villa had lost three key players between seasons. Tom Cleverley, Fabian Delph, and Christian Benteke all moved on. They lost the players who had scored half their Premier League goals! If your captain decides to "look elsewhere" it depresses the whole team.

## Breaking Bad Records

Aston Villa was doing everything wrong at the senior level. McLeish and Lambert managed the club down the drain. Tim Sherwood as manager inherited a team that had lost or drawn its last 21 games. Jack Grealish and the other Villa players landed in the sewerage.

The 2015-2016 season started bad and ended worse. In their first nine games, they were only able to get a single point. The club was one place from the bottom of the league. The board was desperate, so they fired Tim Sherwood. That didn't help much. Sherwood claimed that the club had bought in players with limited talent. The board thought he was just a poor manager. They parted ways in the middle of the season. The board hired Rémi Garde. He couldn't make the changes Villa needed either. He only had three victories in his 147-day stay. They were against Norwich City and Crystal Palace in the league, and Wycombe Wanderers in the FA cup. If one of your three successes is against a League 2 side, then you are scraping the bottom. Your submarine has leaked.

Grealish set a nasty little record for himself that year. He played in 16 matches in which his team lost, one after the other. Sean Thornton lost in 11 matches in a row with Sunderland in 2002-2003. I bet he was glad to stop being the record holder! This started eating away at Jack Grealish's confidence. He was used to being a game-changer in a game-winning side. Now he was in a slump, together with his mates.

Aston Villa only scored 27 goals in the entire Premier League season that year. Jack Grealish scored only one of those. Villa drew eight games and lost 27. They only won three fixtures in the EPL. Aston Villa dropped down to 20th in the league after the 11th weekend of the season. They never moved from there till the end. It was a disaster. As a fan, it is tough to take that. As a player, it's even worse.

The question was, would Jack Grealish be able to take this beating?

## Never Forget Where You Came From

As a professional, you are supposed to look around for better options if things go this badly. But Jack Grealish was not ready to move on from the club he had fought so hard to get into. Tottenham had made a play for him the year before. Leeds United started trying to bargain with Villa to take Grealish off their hands. Villa said no. Jack stayed with the Claret and Blues.

Part of the reason that he had no trouble staying was that there was a £60m release fee in his contract. If Leeds wanted Jack they had to start at £60m. Jack was loyal to his club. His club was also determined to keep him. They would need some exceptional players to get out of this hole. They finally realized how important Jack was for the club's future.

# Falling Off the Bottom of the League

What happens when your club is relegated from the Premier League to the Championship? You lose a lot!

Relegated sides lose half their money! They only get 55% of the money the TV companies pay for covering the football matches—£50m this last season. Fair enough. You aren't giving any entertainment, because you are down in the Championship League. Then, the next year, if you are still down, you only get 45% of the money—£35m. Then the third year you are down, only 20%—£15m. Fewer people come to watch you play—so there is less money from ticket sales. Sponsors don't want you to advertise their products so much any more—so less money there too.

The less money you get, the less you can spend on top players. If you don't have top players, you can't get back up. You could be locked into the lower leagues forever. This was very embarrassing for Villa. It was embarrassing for Villa's fans. And it was embarrassing for Jack and the whole squad. They had to get themselves back up into the Premier League.

Jack Grealish felt he had a job to do. "We're looking to return to the Premier League," he said at the time. "I want to be a big part of that process and will be doing everything possible to make that a reality" (Regan,

2016). Many clubs wanted him. But Grealish wanted to stay. He signed a four-year contract to bind him to the club till 2020. Jack felt like he had been part of the problem. Now he wanted to be part of the solution.

## Sold off Cheap by the Americans

Randy Lerner, Aston Villa's American owner, decided that enough was enough. He had bought the club in 2006 for $125m. But the struggles on the field and behind the scenes were too much for him. As the former owner of the Chicago Bears, he thought an English Premiership Club would be easy to run. It wasn't. The relegation of Villa to the championship was the last straw for him. There's nothing that spells trouble more than an owner who wants to sell your club to somebody else for a $400m loss. Lerner was basically saying that Aston Villa was a lost cause. Jack and the other players wondered what their future held. What was to stop them from eventually joining Notts County in League One? Even worse, could they end up in League Two with Wycombe Wanderers!

So much depended on the new owner, Tony Xia. Xia was super-confident and super-rich. He had great ambitions for the club. He wanted to make Aston Villa one of the top three clubs in the world. That didn't work out. It turned out to be not so simple to make money from a losing club. Xia ploughed in money, but then he ran out of patience and the money stopped rolling into the club. The years of relegation under the ownership of Xia left the club in deep, shall we say, debt. They lost £111,776,896 in 2018-2019.

The men in the boardrooms were obviously struggling. It was up to the players to make Aston Villa shine. Jack Grealish led that charge.

# Chapter 8: Captain Jack

If you are famous, the press does not leave you alone. Anything you do can be a story. The better the story, the more people buy your newspaper. A lot of people wanted to read about Jack Grealish!

It was tough doing interviews. Jack had just seen his beloved club fail at the top level. "Everyone knows this is a club I love dearly," he told a reporter. "It's the place I want to play my football. Bodymoor Heath provides a great environment in which to continue my football education and to call Villa Park home is something I will never take for granted" (Regan, 2016).

That is typical of Jack. He is one of the most talented players in England. He still wanted to "continue his education". If you want to learn, apparently, no one can stop you!

## Fighting in the Championship

In September 2015 Jack finally chose England over Ireland. He seemed to get into his groove as a player. No more inner conflicts. Jack needed all his mental energies for the playing field. He made his choices, and lived with them. England and Aston Villa.

The only way up is through. Jack knew that they had to win the Championship and win it quickly. They had to end in the promotion zone. They set out to play ferociously. Under another new boss, Steve Bruce, Villa started tearing into their Championship opposition.

They say "beware the wounded lion." In the 2016-2017 season, the other Championship teams had to face a snarling Aston Villa. Defences had to cope with Jack Grealish. Villa won five out of their seven pre-season friendlies and looked set to terrorize the lower league.

That is not exactly what happened. It seemed at first as if Villa was going to drop straight through Championship One. Under manager Roberto di Matteo they simply carried on losing. They only won once in their first eleven outings! Grealish scored a goal in that lone victory, but the team was not able to gel. They even lost 2-0 to Preston North End. The Villa management fired di Matteo out of habit and in disgust. Who could stop the rot?

Enter the newest Boss, Steve Bruce. The Villans started winning again. Jonathan Kodjia got into a rich vein of form with 19 of Villa's goals. Grealish chipped in with a next best tally of 5 goals. His main contribution was tearing defences apart with his blazing foot skills. Together they scored more than half of Villa's 47 goals for the season.

So that first season went down OK in the end. Villa finished up in 13th place, about in the middle. The drop stopped. They were floating on an even keel: 16 wins, 16 losses, and 14 draws. Almost exactly average. The question was—were they going up or down the next season?

Villa die-hard fans were worried. Could their team pull out of the Championship? Who would the board sign-on? Money was tight.

## Jack Gets Knocked Back

One of the reasons Jack only scored 5 goals in the 2017-2018 campaign was that he missed so many games. Grealish was knocked out of the entire first half of the season by a freak accident. Jack always played uncompromisingly hard. He dished out tackles, and he could take them in return. He was playing in a routine pre-season friendly against Watford. Somehow he collided weirdly with his old mate Tom Cleverley. Jack went down and didn't get up. He was stretchered off and loaded straight into an ambulance. An hour later he was in surgery.

It was incredibly painful. Blood was leaking everywhere. The doctors had to fix two ugly splits in his kidney. Before he went under anaesthetic, the doctor warned him he might not make it.

Fortunately, the operation was a success.

It changed Jack. He says, "I thought about how everything could be taken away from you in such a short space of time" (Moxley, 2018). He was deeply affected by his brush with death. As he recovered, he worked through a lot of life issues. He realized how important football was to him. "I worked so hard to come back because I missed football. I -wanted to be the best I could be. I was in the gym every day and my energy is so much better. I feel stronger, fitter" (Moxley, 2018).

It took a long time. Jack missed 15 games from August 1 to October. 75 days. It might have been forever, though. Villa was grateful to get him back.

## So, So, So Close

Villa signed John Terry and appointed him to captain the side. It was a great move. This year, at last, the board turned green for Aston Villa. Grealish scored 3 Championship goals as the Villa came roaring back. You don't only measure the value of a midfielder by the number of goals he scores. You also measure him by the number of goals the strikers score off his play. Villa scored 72 goals in 24 wins! Only 11 losses and 11 draws meant that they were in with a chance to play for promotion.

The press started calling Aston Villa "promotion hopefuls". Steve Bruce managed to get their defence organized. They only let through 42 goals in the Championship season. The team was starting to work together again. Jack himself was more deeply committed. A friend said that it was around this time that Jack started turning up on time for practices. His personal life was sorted out. Now he *wanted* to make things work for his club.

On 3 February Grealish scored against Burton Albion in a 3-2 win at Villa Park. The Claret and Blues were on a hot six-game winning streak. Elmohamady played a perfectly weighted cross which Grealish smashed in on the volley. People were noticing Grealish more and more. The opposition had to make special plans to try and keep him quiet. Jack could handle that!

On 7 April 2018 Grealish scored Villa's only goal in a 3-1 loss to Norwich City. It looked like they were going to miss out on automatic promotion. The next week they beat Cardiff City 1-0. That match belonged to Jack Grealish, with his marauding play up the left. He knocked Cardiff City out of the top two with a rocket from 20 yards out. Prince William in the stands seemed quite pleased! They could not get to the top spot, though. Two more wins, a draw, and a loss saw them end the season in fourth place! They would have to scrap for promotion in the play-off dog fight.

It almost went to plan! They beat Middlesbrough 1-0 in the two-leg playoff. Then they went down 0-1 to Fulham in the final. Fulham went through. Villa stayed behind. It was heartbreaking for the Villa squad and the Villa fans.

Time and money were running out. Aston Villa had one more season to get back up into the Premier League.

## Fractured Jack

The new season started off poorly. Villa seemed to have pulled itself into its shell again. In the 11th match of the season, they let lowly Preston North End catch them up for a 3-3 draw. The team was down to 12th place in the league. Somebody threw a cabbage at Steve Bruce. Aston Villa sacked him and brought in Dean Smith. What could he do?

It seemed at first that he couldn't do much. Villa lost against Millwall. Then they beat Swansea City and then lost twice in a row to Norwich City and Queens Park Rangers. But then they started to win again. They went down as low as 16, but were soon up to number 8 and rising.

Then Jack Grealish got injured again.

By now Jack was crucial to Villa's plans for promotion. His days playing Gaelic football made him really tough, but not tough enough. Something happened to him during the 1-0 win over Swansea. Typical Jack, he kept right on playing. He played on for 7 weeks-on painkillers! While trying to hide his hobbling, he scored a great early goal against Bolton Wanderers. He scored another against Birmingham City. He explains that in the end the pain simply got too much. He was substituted off 10 minutes from full-time in a match against West Brom. It turned out to be a stress fracture of the tibia! He was out for 83 days. All he could do was spend time in the gym putting on a bit more upper body muscle.

Warning! If you are scared of leg injuries, do not play football!

The problem with the shin is that there is so little muscle on it. The impact goes almost directly from boot to bone. If you have played football at all, you know this. Shin splints are one common footballer's shin injury. That's where the calf muscle pulls the bones apart, and you get a lot of swelling and pain. Jack thought he had that. He didn't. Another common injury is a stress fracture. After being kicked too many times you can get a microscopic break in the bone. Lots of people had kicked Jack Grealish. He was out for 12 weeks.

Meanwhile, Villa fans were chewing their nails as their team only just held its place on the table. Grealish missed 13 games. The team hovered around 10th place. It looked like their season was going to end in an average, middle of the league position.

Then Jack came back!

# Jack Grealish Gets the Armband

Jack came off the injury list two days before a clash with Derby County, set for 2 March 2019. Then manager Dean Smith made one of the best decisions in recent Aston Villa history. He gave Jack the Captain's armband! Smith sprung the news on Grealish on Friday 1 March. The team had suffered without him. Now the Boss decided to go all in. They needed a miracle, and the only miracle man they had was Jack Grealish.

Jack was ecstatic. His dream had come in stages. He had worked really hard. Now here he was: not only a permanent first team member but captain! He led his team out that day in front of about 35,000 Villa fans, including his dad. Magic.

Jack Grealish was at his stylish, unstoppable best. His opponents hardly knew what hit them. Hourihane scored early: 1-0 to Villa. Then, in the ten minutes before halftime, Abraham scored. Hourihane scored another. So did Grealish (in extra time). That onslaught completely broke Derby County. Grealish had opened up the field for Abraham's shot, and Hourihane scored off the rebound for his second. The attack pack was working together to perfection. Derby County never recovered, and the game ended 4-0. Cap'n Jack was smiling! His first day back and his first day as captain was one big celebration. When he was substituted 10 minutes from the final whistle the crowd rose to their feet to cheer their boy.

The miracles kept coming that year.

The match against Derby County was the first of a ten-win streak under Grealish's captaincy. The next week Grealish scored the goal that beat Birmingham City 1-0. They beat Nottingham Forest, Middlesbrough, and Blackburn Rovers. They swatted off Sheffield Wednesday and Rotherham United. Grealish scored again against Rotherham. Abraham, Kodjia, and Hourihane headed the goal-scoring chart that season. Grealish came in at Joint fourth with John McGinn with 6 goals apiece. That is even with missing half the season!

The wins kept coming. Bristol City, Bolton Wanderers, Millwall. Villa seemed unstoppable. The fans were delirious about Jack Grealish. The crowds gave him the highest honor—his own song!

*Super, super Jack!*

*Super, super Jack!*

*Super, super Jack!*

*Super attacking Grealish*

Villa finished the season in fifth place. Back in the scrap for promotion. It had all been under Jack Grealish's spell. Could the magic hold?

# Learning to Lead

Aston Villa was on the brink again. Jack was a magician, yes, but he was more than that. Through the extreme pressure he had faced, he had become a leader. He was still only 23. He was a friendly and highly intelligent footballer. He had good people skills to match his scintillating football skills. People liked and respected him. They trusted him and expected a lot from him.

We can see how much he had grown in the incident of the pitch invader. On Sunday 10 March 2019, the Villans were playing away against Birmingham City. Grealish was completely focused on the game. Then this big thug with a flat cap hops onto the field, dodges the security, and punches Jack in the side of the head! Grealish went down hard! Then things almost went really badly for the invader. First, the Villans mobbed him. Then the Birmingham City team poured in too. You might not like Aston Villa, but Jack was a Brummie! The police managed to wrestle their way in to the invader, who must have been wetting his pants. They led him off before he got too badly injured. He got 14 weeks in prison.

How did Jack react? Calmly, and with good humor. He did not try to put the boot in. He just gathered his thoughts and regained his focus. He went on with his usual game. In the second half, he made a way for himself inside the penalty area and smashed home the winner for Aston Villa. That's the man. Grealish was totally focused on the team winning. You can follow a captain like that.

# Chapter 9: Promotion: Getting Up and Hanging On

Grealish led Villa in the record ten-game winning streak. This extraordinary feat had got the team to the brink of promotion. Only two more games stood between success and failure! Last year they failed at this point. Could Jack Grealish haul the Claret and Blues over this last hurdle?

## Up the Down Ladder: Playoff Semi-Finals

West Bromwich Albion was the first target. As usual, the playoff semi-final was played over two legs. This year the first was at Villa Park.

The atmosphere in the stands is dynamic. The Baggies kick-off, and almost immediately Grealish is driven off the ball onto the ground. In the 4th minute, Whelan heads a cross from Grealish over the bar. Villans groan in the stands.

The pace is quick. The play seesaws from one end to the other. Then Whelan fluffs a pass, and Gayle pinches it. He slams the ball into the right of the net, past Steer's fingertips. West Bromwich Albion 1—Aston Villa 0. West Bromwich Albion has not lost a single match so far this season after taking the lead!

Villa is using its possession advantage to pepper the goal-but the shots are all frustratingly wide. The passes aren't quite reaching their targets. The stands are quiet. 5 minutes of extra time. Nothing. Villa goes in at halftime to face Dean Smith 1-0 down.

Whatever he said in the locker room, Villa comes out energized. They still dominate possession but now things start to look ominous for the Baggies. Grealish is an ever-present menace. In the 75th minute, Jack dribbles through and passes the ball back for Hurricane Hourihane. Hourihane smashes the ball from 25 yards past the WBA goalie. 1-1! Three minutes later, Gibbs trips Grealish in the penalty box. Abraham coolly strokes the ball into the bottom right from the spot. And that's it. Villa goes into the second leg a goal up.

Three days later, and it's the second leg of the semi-finals at the Hawthorns. The crowd is not welcoming, but Jack and the boys are used to that. Once again Villa is the king of possession (74%), and lead the Baggies by 24 shots on goal to 10. Nothing goes in. Craig Dawson's 29th-minute goal brings West Bromwich Albion up equal to Villa on aggregate, 2-2. Villa miss and miss and miss. Their traveling fans are frantic with worry. Then the Baggies' captain, Chris Brunt gets sent off. They keep their heads. 6 minutes of extra time are added on. Villa throws themselves furiously against the ten-man opponents. Hammer, hammer, hammer, but they still can't get through. So it's on to 30 minutes of extra time, with two exhausted sides. Nothing doing. A minute is added to the first 15 minutes. Still nothing. Nothing in the second 15 minutes. Three minutes is added. Villa cannot break the deadlock.

So it all comes down to penalties. Jack Grealish's team will go up or down depending on the final showdown between goalie and shooter.

Dean Smith had been working on penalties for four weeks. Jed Steer, the goalie, had been studying the shooting statistics of every West Brom player. Now, all that work was going to be put to the test. The Baggies won the toss and were up first.

Mason Holgate drives hard into the left of the net. Jed Steer is in the way-he guesses right! West Brom, 0-0. Connor Hourihane outfoxes Sam Johnstone and slips the ball into an empty corner. Villa up 1-0!

Ahmed Hegazi steps up and Steer saves again! He gets a steel bar of an arm to Hegazi's shot to the right! 1-0 to Villa! Dean Smith had made sure Mile Jedinak was on the field for this. He does not disappoint. He expertly finds the net. 2-0 to Villa!

Tosin Adarabioyo side-foots it in. West Brom are back at 2-1 down. Jack Grealish makes no mistake. He sends Johnstone the wrong way. Even the goalie's catlike mid-air twist can only leave him spectating the bulging net. Villa 3-1 up and looking set to win!

Kieran Gibbs scores for West Brom. Villa's lead was down to 3-2. But Albert Adomah could win it for Villa. He misses! The shot goes into orbit over the crossbar! Villa fans are biting their scarves!

James Morrison puts another one past Steer-all square at 3-3. This could be West Bromwich Albion into the Final. Tammy Abraham strolls up. His 1.9m (6'3") frame unwinds with all the spring-loaded power available to him. He unleashes a dinky little side-footed push. Johnstone gets a toe to it, but it trickles in—GOAL! The Claret and Blues are through!

It's a bitter disappointment for West Brom. But the brilliant Villans deserve their success.

Jack was really proud of his team. His mind, though, was already on the finals. And last year's disappointment was keeping him focused. "We done it last season," he told reporters, "but it's no good going on the run that we have been on and falling at the final hurdle. We'll have a few days off and then prepare for Wembley" (Fisher, 2019).

# His Royal Highness the Worried Fan

Then came Derby County. They were up against an Aston Villa side with captain Jack Grealish at his searing best.

Both sides studied their opponents that week. They viewed endless videos. They discussed their opponent's strengths and weaknesses. They laid plans. The Physios had repaired and taped all the broken bits. The sides were ready for each other.

The day dawned, 27 May 2019. The crowds started to cram into Wembley stadium. The bodyguards in their dark glasses ushered HRH the Prince of Wales into the royal box. He was hoping he would not have to give the trophy over to the opposition again. Kevin Grealish, Jack's dad, settled in amongst a mass of Villa Fans. The players finished their last preparations. Jack Grealish gave his team the final captain's word. Then they were on the field in front of about 86,000 berserk fans.

The teams lined up for the National Anthem. The commentators went on about how the winner would get £170m in broadcast fees. But Jack just wanted to get his team back into the Premier League.

Kickoff, Aston Villa.

Jack Grealish led the charge.

Aston Villa strikes hard and early. Hourihane and El Ghazi and Tuanzebe are so close! Grealish shoots over the bar. El Ghazi forces a corner. McGinn forces another corner. McGinn shoots wide. Villa can't land the blow!

Then the Rams rally. El Ghazi sees yellow. Wilson and Bennet start to get the ball moving forward for Derby. Abraham gets the ball in the box. He turns and kicks, but the ball flies high. El Ghazi brings it too close for comfort, but Derby clears its line. Back up the other side Jed Steer engulfs a wicked drive straight into his midriff from Mount. Derby win the first of their five corners, but Keogh heads the ball over the bar. Villa works the ball upfield. El Mahomedy hangs a delicious cross just ahead of El Ghazi. El Ghazi is onside. He rises to meet the ball and heads it in! GOOOOOAL!

One more minute is added on, but the first half closes with Villa ahead by 1-0. Wembley stands are a seething cauldron. *"Super, super Jack!"* roars out. The Rams fans come back with *"Always look on the bright side, alright!"*

Referee Damir Skomina from Slovenia blows the whistle for the second half.

Derby County comes out looking dangerous. Three yellows are awarded as the sides exchange fouls. Roos, the Ram's goalie, only just snags a ball from the 1.96m Tyrone Mings. It's close. It was a perfect free kick by Hourihane. Villa presses forward hard. El Ghazi fires in a hard shot. It gets deflected and Roos gets the angle wrong. In a horrendous error, he tries to catch the high deflection. He misses! McGinn taps it in! Villa fans explode: *"We've got McGinn, super John McGinn, I just don't think you understand!"* Jack Grealish's boys are doing their job.

Derby County has ten minutes to pull two back. Nine minutes. And Marriott scores for Derby! Mings hurts himself intercepting Waghorn. The ball bobs around and Marriot hammers one in through everybody's legs! It touches Waghorn on the way, so he gets the goal. But nobody is worried about who gets the credit. Can Villa weather the desperate Derby storm?

Eight minutes. Prince William is looking as nervous as a royal is allowed to. The bodyguards are not paying attention to the play—they must all be rugby fans. Seven minutes. Six minutes. Jack has got everyone in the team absolutely focused. Five. Four. Three. Two. Seven minutes of extra time are added to the clock! Stress for the Claret and Blues, desperation for the Rams. Fans are having asthma attacks. The minutes crawl around the clock. Grealish is a frenzied blur on the field.

The final whistle!

Aston Villa are going through! Half the crowd falls silent. The other half are jubilant. The Claret and Blues are back in the Premier League! Top-flight football is coming back to Villa Park.

Rotherham, Bolton, and Ipswich fall down to the Championship. Norwich City, Sheffield United, and Aston Villa take their place at the top.

The last word needs to go to Grealish. "When I look around and I've got John McGinn, Tammy and Anwar, I feel like we can beat anyone. I can't describe how happy I am" (Maltby, 2019).

# Chapter 10: Jack Grealish—Villa's Houdini

Houdini was a famous magician. He specialized in escaping from impossible situations. Jack Grealish could have acted on the same stage!

## Tax Man: "Pay up or Go Out of Business!"

Was there going to be any money, though? Villa owed £4m to the tax man. If they couldn't pay, they might have to sell Villa Park! It might be the end of the club!

That is where Sawiris and Edens as the new owners came to the party. Tony Xia had lost interest. So the new partnership paid off Xia's £30m debt to Lerner, the previous owner. They paid another £30m to get control of the club. They also paid off that dangerous £4m debt.

Sawiris and Edens had bought Villa for a song. Now the fans could keep on singing!

# Villans Fight On: UP THE VILLA!

It's one thing to get into the Premier League. It's another thing to stay there! It's often a revolving door down at the bottom of the league. If you can't latch on and haul yourself up, down you go again! The 2019-2020 season was tough for Villa. They needed a captain who could handle the rough stuff. Jack Grealish had scars and thick skin. He knew personally how to fight desperate battles.

The 2019-2020 season was the strangest season on record. Villa needed leadership that could cope with "strange." Jack was their man.

They started off the season OK. Four losses, three wins, and two draws. Grealish scored in Villa's 5-1 rout of Norwich City at Carrow Road, and again in Villa's 2-1 win over the Seagulls. That left them at 15 in the league. Not brilliant. Jack's team, though, was heading into deeper trouble.

Villa was outgunned that season. Grealish had 36 appearances and scored 8 goals. That was good. What was bad was that he was the team's top scorer! Villa only scored 41 goals in the Premier League. They let through 67! Grealish was playing some of his best football. His teammates were not. Their ace striker, McGinn, got injured in December. It put him out for the rest of the season. Villa was losing and losing and losing.

The reason they did not do worse was that Jack Grealish was so outstanding. He scored in a draw against Manchester United. He scored Villa's only goal when the Claret and Blues were bled dry, 4-1, by Leicester City. He scored one goal in a 3-1 loss to Southampton. Jack added a first-half goal to Wesley's as they beat Burnley 2-1. Manchester City slaughtered the Villans 6-1. Jack scored the only goal for his club. He scored an equalizer against the Seagulls. After 30 games, Aston Villa was down at 19. They looked like staying in the relegation red zone. On 9 March 2020 Villa lost abjectly to Leicester City, 4-0.

Villa fans were in shock. They went home and never came back.

## Empty Stands!

Covid 19 hit. Hospitals started filling up. Oxygen started running low for patients. The EFL shut down its season on 13 March 2020. Villa had to slink off and lick its wounds. They came back scarred but healed.

Training in small groups was allowed again on 19 May. On 27 May they started playing practice matches. On 17 June the Premier League was back. Without the fans.

Home-ground advantage is a real thing! During the Behind closed doors days of football, teams won a much lower percentage of their home games. It wasn't much fun. No songs. Villa fans had a sulky season at home watching the games on the telly. TV sets got broken by flying cabbages. In front of silent stands, Jack and the boys struggled on.

## Jack Grealish: Escape Artist

It was just like the bad old days before relegation! Aston Villa was down in 19th position. Ten winless weeks bit back at Jack's 10-win series of the last season. But Jack had been there before. This time he was captain. He was determined to pull his team through. He knew he could do it again!

The last four matches of that season were epic! Position 17 was still the place of safety. Teams at 18, 19, and 20 were on the relegation trapdoor. Once again, Villa was fighting for 17th place. This time they had to get there without their mighty army of supporters.

Match 35. 12 July against Crystal Palace. Sakho scores first for the Glaziers, but there's a tricep involved. Goal disallowed. Fans at home cheer the VAR! Jack is at his panic-inducing best. The players are feeling the midsummer heat. Everybody else's pace slows down, but Jack seems to speed up! It gets to 4 minutes into extra time before Trezeguet stabs in a free-kick from Hourihane. GOAL! Villa up 1-0 at the break. Then Van

Aanhold brings Grealish down in the box. VAR rules that Grealish started it. The penalty is reversed. Villa fans are suddenly not happy with VAR anymore. Villa are pushing strongly, now, and Palace has no answer. Grealish plays Samatta in, who fires off a missile on target. Guaita saves! Trezeguet picks up the loose ball and stabs it in under the goalie! GOOOOAL! Villa gooe 2-0 up and keeps the lead to full time. But they are still stuck at 19th place.

Match 36. 16 July and Aston Villa take on Everton. Aston Villa think they've got it with Konsa's 72nd-minute goal. But Walcott spoils their party with an equalizer three minutes from time. It ends 1-1, and Villa stays at 19, with only 180 minutes left in the season.

Match 37. It does not get any easier. On 21 July they are down to play the powerful Arsenal. The Gunners dominate the play. They have about 70% of possession and put together more than 600 passes. Villa only makes 264 passes. But the crucial pass is a corner nod-down from Mings to Trezeguet, who SCORES in the 27th minute! Aston Villa has downed the Mighty Gunners! They are one place above relegation. Furniture gets broken all across Birmingham as Villans fans jump around living rooms in excitement! Jack's men have only one match to go.

Match 38. 26 July. It's the last match of the Premier League season. If Villa loses this one, they are in the relegation zone. A win will see them safe. A draw will be fine if Arsenal can manage to beat Watford. Things are that close! Their opponents for the day: West Ham United. But the Hammers are coming off a flaming hot six-match winning streak. The Villans have only scrambled their way to the end.

The Villa are playing in their Green and Black away strip. Villa fans are not supporting the Claret and Blue today!

The Hammers take the kick-off. Jack Grealish leads his men into action. The first half is nervy and flat. Even McGinn can't make anything happen. In the silent stadium you can hear the managers shouting, and the thud of boot on ball. The only spectators are the substitutes and the press. It's 0-0 at the water break. The sides finish 0-0 at halftime.

Tension mounts around thousands of TV sets as the halftime commercials play. Thousands of toilets flush at the same time. Fans squeeze back into couches. Referee Michael Oliver sets Villa's last 45 minutes of the season going.

The stalemate continues. Grealish pushes the attack up the left. West Ham resists and probes up the middle. A Fredericks strike for West Ham deflects off one of his own players. A freekickfor fouling Grealish is headed over by Samatta. It starts to rain. Yarmalenko hits the side netting for the Hammers. Grealish takes a freekick. He bruises the wall, but the wall holds. Grealish finds McGinn who gets it back to Grealish. But he fires wide. Lanzini hits the Villa wall with a

Hammers free-kick. Now we're into the final ten minutes.

Davis misses. Villa fans groan.

McGinn finds Grealish. He smashes it in left-footed! GOOOOAL! All the fans at home relax. Looks like Jack has done it again.

But the drama isn't over. The next minute Yarmolenko unleashes a powerful shot at the other end. It ricochets off Grealish. The deflection bounces unkindly over the Villa goal line! 1-1 in the final 5 minutes of play! Villa fans are now crouching behind their couches. Villa sticks like glue to their opponents. The final whistle goes!

A few more results need to come in. Meanwhile, Jack is awarded the undisputed man of the match. How did Watford fare against Arsenal? The result comes in. Arsenal has beaten Watford 3-2! Villa keep their 17th place and live to fight another season in the Premiership! They have beaten Bournemouth and Watford by a single point! If they had lost they would have gone down on goal difference! Villa's absent fans could sleep in peace for the rest of the summer.

The fans and the players voted Jack Grealish player of the season.

Villa's fans know their football. They deeply admired Jack's leadership and commitment. They knew, however, that their team had the potential to be pushing the top teams. It showed in the EFL Cup, where Villa powered their way through to the 2020 final. They showed unstoppable talent. They thrashed Crewe Alexandra 6-1. Grealish helped himself to one of those. They beat the Seagulls 3-1. Jack also got a goal that day. Villa eased past Wolverhampton Wanderers 2-1. Aston Villa demolished Liverpool 5-0 to reach the semifinals. Grealish was on the bench that day with a niggle. His mates managed fine without him. Then came the two-leg semi-finals. They fought hard for a 3-2 aggregate victory over Leicester City. In the finals, though, they ran into the powerful Manchester City and came out 2-1 short.

## Going up Further!

Management at Villa Park had to make better plans for the 2020-2021 season. They wanted the trophy, not 17th place. The first step: make sure you keep Jack Grealish. So they signed him up for a five-year contract. Anybody who wanted Jack would have to pay £60,000,000 just to open up talks about his price. To be honest, though, Jack was not going anywhere. Aston Villa was his first love. He was up and running for the 2020-2021 season.

Villa started by winning 4 games on the trot. Sheffield United, Fulham, and Leicester City got mown down. Liverpool fans were horrified when Mighty Liverpool lost 7-2 to Villa. Grealish did not miss out on the goal feast.

Aston Villa was in the top half of the league for most of the season. It was a fighting performance, much better than 2019-2020.

Covid 19 was not over yet. The match against Everton on 16 January had to be postponed. Too many of the Villa first team caught the virus at Bodymoor Heath.

In February 2020 Jack injured his shin, again. He had to miss 12 matches. With Jack sidelined out, Villa won 3, drew 4, and lost 5 matches. They obviously missed their inspirational captain.

Villa eventually got its fans back in 2021! For the last two weeks of Premier League football, 10,000 fans were allowed in the stands. "*Super Jack*" was back!

Jack Grealish's Aston Villa finished at 11 in the table in 2020-2021! This was not where they wanted to be. It is also not where they *didn't* want to be! After starting at the bottom end of the league they won more matches than they lost (16 wins, 7 draws, and 7 losses).

## Diving Diva or Foul Magnet?

Not everybody likes Jack Grealish. Some say he's a diver. That's mostly jealousy. Nobody would turn him

> **Comment [SK]:** Need changing?

away if he wanted to sign up. Some Irish fans say bitter things about him, out of disappointment. Nobody doubts his talent, though.

Jack also gets lots of hostility on the field. He humiliates defenders as he runs through them. Then they kick him. In 2018-2019, Jack Grealish drew 149 tackles. That's even with him being out for three months with a shin injury. In 2019-2020, Grealish was fouled a record 167 times!

## Bad Boy Jack

Of course, Jack has been known to dive a *little*. His only red card has been a second yellow for diving. On field Jack generally picks up very few cards. He has only got that one red card, a second yellow for diving in a 2-0 win against West Bromwich Albion. We don't like him because he's perfect. We like him because he's Jack!

Jack partied with his friends. There is no problem with partying. Having fun is usually fine. An elite athlete, though, has to be expertly tuned. The slightest tinge of a hangover could lose him his edge. He would still be as good as the best players he was coming up against. But he needed to be *better* than them. Jack's value to a team is that he is better than his opponents.

Some of Jack's friends couldn't understand this. *They* had nothing to lose if they got hammered on a Saturday night. They were only going to stay at home, sleep late, and watch the telly the next day with a slight headache. But Jack was going to have to *play*. He did not want to send a message to his mates that they were not important anymore. But in order to be at the top of his game, he had to party less. Many of his friends could not accept that. Sadly, Jack had to stop hanging out with friends who pushed him to drink heavily.

Alcohol calms you down. It's a chemical that slows you down and helps you relax. Jack on attack did not need calming down!

In another way, he did need calming down, but alcohol wouldn't help. Jack had to learn to control his temper. Sometimes people pushed him, so he would push back. He admitted to putting the studs into Conor Coady. It was in a bad-tempered draw played out against Wolverhampton Wanderers in October 2016. This was only picked up after the match. Officials received video footage and complaints. It went to the FA Disciplinary Panel as a charge of stamping, and Grealish was banned for the next three games. Harsh but fair. Jack has never been cited since. He learned from his mistake.

After a depressing loss to Everton (4-0!) Jack went out with friends to a nightclub and drank heavily. With the team in such trouble, the manager, Remi Garde, had been warning his players to focus. He told his squad to have a quiet Christmas and not to party. So when the papers splashed pictures of Jack at a club, Garde was furious! He sent him to train with the Academy players. The message: "If you act like a kid, you can play with the kids." Garde was aware that fans wanted to know why Grealish was not taking the crisis seriously. It seemed to work. Jack came back to the squad with a much better attitude.

Also, being good at football does not stop you from being stupid sometimes! But Jack has always taken his punishment and paid his fines. Then he refocuses and produces more brilliance for his club.

And the English selectors had not forgotten this fireball of a player!

# Chapter 11: England's Fan Favorite

Grealish's International career was taking off at the same time. The selectors were watching the way he dealt with the drama at Villa. They liked him more and more for the national squads.

Villa was sacking managers every few months. Jack wanted to play football. He chose to come back to international football, and he confirmed his choice of England in September 2015. "I am English, my parents were born in England," he explained. "I was obviously born in England, so I feel English" (Preece, 2021).

Jack started going up for England as Villa was going down on the Premier League table.

## Jack's Early English Career

Jack played against Portugal in his first match for England under-21s. He came in for the last 18 minutes of the game on 19 May 2016. Gareth Southgate, the under-21s manager, made sure Grealish was on his squad for the Toulon Tournament. Irish eyes were scowling; he had already played six times for the

Republic of Ireland under-21s. Everyone *wanted* Grealish. But only Grealish *owned* Grealish.

Four days later Southgate handed him his first start. England was up against Guinea and beat them emphatically, 7-1. Guinea scored first with a scrambled goal. Then Jack volleyed in a weak clearance to level the scores. Ward-Prowse and Redmond scored. Then Redmond dinked the ball onto Jack Grealish's right foot and he slammed it in. More goals followed as the Three Lions won 7-1. England went on to take the cup home. Jack Grealish was now sure of his place.

His next outing for the England under-21s was against Bosnia & Herzegovina on 11 October 2016. England won 5-0. He played against France on 14 November, a match England lost 3-2. He played on 27 March the next year in a 4-0 victory over Denmark. Then he turned 21. He had played under-21 International football for two countries for four years.

Now it was time to represent England in the senior team.

On 31 August 2020 he got his first National call-up for two UEFA League games: against Iceland and Denmark. On 8 September he got 14 minutes for England off the bench against Denmark. "I always wanted to play for England," he said. "The UEFA Nations League fixture was where my dream met reality!"

# UEFA Euro 2020 (2021)

Covid 19 changed all our lives. It stopped the 2020 Olympics. It also stopped the UEFA Euro 2020 tournament. The next year, though, the English selectors put together another squad. UEFA Euro 2020 was going to be played in 2021. It would be played at only 11 very big stadiums. This made it easier to control the risk of catching Covid 19. They still called it "Euro 2020," though. They didn't want to print all the flags and t-shirts again!

Jack Grealish was on the England list.

England mostly brushed aside the smaller nations in the qualifying rounds. They did lose to the Czech Republic 2-1 in October 2019, and to Denmark and Belgium once each in the Nations League. They qualified by beating Denmark.

England was kitted up and ready when Euro 2020 kicked off on 11 June 2021.

England shared group D with Croatia, the Czech Republic, and Scotland. All the group D matches were scheduled for Wembley Stadium.

The fans were trying hard to get to the matches, but Covid 19 was making that difficult. They were only allowed to sell 22,500 tickets by lottery. Then, to get in you had to have a vaccine card and a negative Covid test. In the end, only about 18,000 fans were there to watch. It was sad to see so much red seating at Wembley.

England's opening match was against Croatia on 13 June.

The roof is open, and the sun is shining at Wembley. The whistle blows, and England's campaign begins. England looks impressive, and Croatia looks overwhelmed. No one is buying that, though. Croatia has sunk English hopes before. Half time comes, and the sides are locked at 0-0. In the second half the contest continues. At one stage Jack gets up and warms up, and the crowd goes wild. But then he sits down again. The crowd subsides. Then Sterling takes one through the middle. He fires off a shot that just tips the goalie's fingers as it bends in. GOAL! England go 1-0 up in the 57th minute! Can they keep ahead? Harry Kane shoots a cross wide and hits the post with his ribs with a bone-rattling slide. Croatia hits and misses. England wins. Grealish looks on wistfully from the substitute's bench.

Game 2 of group D brought Scotland down South for a fourth match. It was very wet underfoot. Wembley has the same red seats showing and the same tiny crowd. Lots of Scots fans in kilts. England fans in white. No goals come in the first half. Both sides shoot and miss. This time Grealish gets a run, subbing on at the one-hour mark. It's Villa's Grealish against Villa's McGinn. They cancel each other out. The match ends in a goalless draw.

So, Game 3 was the decider of who would lead the group. Match day 3 for England and the Czech Republic was on 22 June. A measly 19,000 fans sprinkle the red seats at Wembley. This time Grealish is in Southgate's starting lineup. Southgate has been under pressure for the defensive tactics against Scotland. Well, if you want an attack, call on Jack! England comes in like a wrecking ball. In the twelfth minute, Saka brings the ball expertly up-field. He gets the ball to Grealish, who sends the perfect cross to Raheem Sterling. Sterling SCORES! Fans in front of TV screens go wild! Fans in the stands jump on each other. Then comes the grind of staying ahead. It turns into a Grealish-Saka show, and the Czech Republic gets nothing back. England tops the group table and move on.

## Super, Super-Sub Jack

Every English fan tuned in for the next day's Group F game between Hungary and Germany. Who would England prefer to play? Hungary, without a doubt. For 55 years Germany has knocked England out whenever they have met in knockout football.

Hungary and Germany play to a 2-2 draw. England *will* face Germany in the final 16!

The day dawns. Double the number of fans make their way through the Wembley turnstiles. There are 40,000 people in, about half full. The sides sing the National Anthems. Badly. These men are not the first pick for the church choir! Both teams take a knee against racism. And Danny Makkelie blows the whistle!

Wait! They are starting without Foden, Mount, or Grealish. Is Southgate trying to *defend* the Germans from an English victory? defeat the Germans by defending the entire match?

England does defend well. Germany probes and picks away. Nothing gets through. On the nine-minute mark, Rice fouls on the edge of his own box. Havertz smashes the ball at the Three Lions wall. Everything holds, and Rice gets the bruise. Fair punishment for his lack of discipline! Stones gets the ball on his head from a freekick minutes later, but Germany is clear. Sterling shoots—blocked. McGuire shoots—saved. Saka is menacing down the right touchline. Attack is met by defence. Defence is met by attack. Harry Kane misses again. He has touched the ball nine times, with no result.

After 45+1 minutes, halftime brings a breather. Both of England's midfielders are on yellow cards. Both teams need to work out their tactics for the next half. England's fans are praying that that will include Grealish!

The second half opens with Germany building methodically from the back. Pickford, the English goalie, just manages to tip a vicious shot from Havertz over the bar! 67 minutes have gone by and neither side is winning. Time at last for some attacking strategy! Saka comes off and Grealish goes on! English fans make it clear what they want Grealish to do. And he does it!

Time moves on to 75 minutes. England builds up another move. Sterling. Kane. Grealish. Shaw out wide and sends in a cross. This time Sterling latches on and SCORES FOR ENGLAND! Fans explode in Wembley Stadium and all around England! 20.6 million fans were watching on BBC1!

Another German freekick gets blocked by England's unflinching wall. England has shaken off their fear. 80 minutes pass by, and Muller shoots wide! 85 minutes. Can England hold? They can do better than that! On 87 minutes Shaw brings the ball forward in the middle. Out it goes to Grealish on the left. Grealish sends in a low cross, and Harry Kane SCORES! England up 2-0 over Germany in the quarter-finals! It's a berserk moment that will live forever in every fan's memory!

Now for the last anxious moments of the match. Germany charges recklessly at the English. They get close, but England holds firm. They send high ball after high ball through. England calmly fields the bombs and sends them back upfield. Six minutes of extra time unfold slowly. Desperate Germany meets determined England. The final whistle blows.

England has beaten Germany in a knockout match! The English fans celebrated in the rain till late that night.

## Reaching Out for Euro Glory

It seemed like nothing could stop England.

Ukraine beat Sweden that day. So they pressed on to meet England at the Stadio Olimpico on 3 July 2021. Switzerland was to play Spain. Belgium was down to play Italy, and the Czech Republic had Denmark to face. The last eight.

Grealish's mates did not need him on the day. The Ukrainians ran into the Three Lions at their most savage. England chewed them up and spit them out in a 4-0 mauling. Harry Kane scored two, McGuire and Henderson got one each. Jack Grealish looked on peacefully from the substitute bench. It became clear that SouthGate was using Jack as an impact player. When the Boss needed a breakthrough, he'd bring on his breakthrough man.

The quarter-finals ended with four teams standing. Italy, Spain, Denmark, and England.

*"It's coming home, it's coming home, it's coming, Football's coming home!"* The fans were beginning to

believe their song. Only three teams could stop them. Denmark was the first.

Spain was playing Italy. England was facing Denmark.

# One Hand On the Cup

The England Denmark match was down for Wednesday, 7 July. The venue, Wembley again.

Almost 65,000 fans got into Wembley that day. It wasn't full, but there was a decent crowd at last. England's Prime Minister and Prince William got free seats. England was filled with red cross flags and three lion pennants.

The teams did their footballing best with the national anthems. England got a *lot* of help singing *God Save the Queen*! Then it's down to work. Not for Jack, though. He sits impatiently on the bench. The super-sub is waiting.

England comes out hard. Denmark is on the back foot for the first ten minutes. Most of the play is in the Danish half. Then they steady themselves. Pickford, England's goalie has to punch out a brilliant shot. The Danes start to win the ball and keep it, and the English fans become uneasy. The English are making the Danish goalie work really hard on the counter attack, though. But now Dolberg snakes forward and Mount knocks him down. Freekick Denmark, 35 yards out! And Damsgaard scores!

55,000 English fans all choke on their drink.

It's a brutal beauty of a shot, over the wall and dipping under the bar. Pickford didn't see it coming. Did the Danish wall block his line of sight? Jack Grealish puts his head in his hands.

Now to see whether England has big-match steel. Schmeichel, the Danish goalie, pulls off a desperate save. He leaves the goal mouth open. Then Saka fizzes a ball across the goalmouth. Sterling and Kjaer tangle up with each other at high velocity. Body parts are everywhere. And Kjaer SCORES AN OWN GOAL! The English fans go bananas. The Danish fans groan. But there it is. England is now level 1-1 with Denmark. Job done for now. 45 minutes to go.

England resumes after halftime with an unchanged side. Jack is squirming on the bench.

The play is uncompromising. Pickford has to fly to keep the ball out. The Danes are holding nothing back. England's midfield is a little soft. Shots pour in. England breaks and threatens the Danish goal. Nothing doing. Players start to tire. Denmark substitutes on three fresh players.

And on comes Grealish at last!

The Danes mark Grealish as tightly as they can. Then Kane gets fouled in the Danish box! No penalty, says

VAR. The two sides are fighting each other to a standstill. Full time comes and goes, and six minutes are added. Grealish cannot unlock the door. England has all the ball but nothing works. Extra time it has to be.

Southgate gets his boys in a huddle. They decide on a plan and take it to the Danes. The Danes absorb the shock. England brings on Henderson and Foden. England besieges the Danish six-yard box. The fans start to roar out *"It's coming home!"* The Danish look as though they are on the ropes. It's over 100 minutes. Sterling goes down in the box! VAR upholds the penalty!

It all comes down to this.

Kane steps up. The tension is immense. Harry Kane, Harry Kane, Harry Kane!

He sidefoots it weakly to the left of the goalie, and Schmeichel saves! The Danes explode! But the ball bounces out of Schmeichel's grasp and Kane nails it on the rebound! GOAL TO ENGLAND!!!!!!

The Danes contract and the English expand. Wembley becomes the epicenter of an English celebration that rocks the islands. But can they keep the lead?

Half of the extra time comes and goes. Then Grealish gets *subbed off* for Trippier! This has never happened to an English sub before! He has helped England to move forward with relentless pressure. They have taken the lead. Now Southgate packs away his fighter jet and pulls out his tank. Trippier dribbles the ball by himself around empty corners of the park. The Danes blow a fuse trying to get the ball and use it. England shuts down their every move.

The full-time whistle blows! Jack joins his mates in celebration. England has won 2-1.

The fans went home singing:

*"We've got Jacky Jack Grealish, we've got Kane.*

*We've got Jude, Rice, and Foden, we will reign.*

*We've got Stones and Harry Maguire, the England are on fire.*

*Mounty scores for England once again!"* (ProLyrical, 2022)

## Penalty Drama at UEFA Euro Final

England had reached the final for the first time in 55 years! The whole of England was flying the flag. Even the Coldstream Guards played *"It's Coming Home."* Around the world, 328 million people found the sports channel. More than 65,000 people had a ticket for Wembley in their hands. Everybody remembers 11 July 2021.

Technicians set up the cameras for the Video Assisted Referee system (VAR). Somebody polished Prince William's shoes. Everything was ready.

It was a painful day if you are an England fan, so I will make it quick. Luke Shaw scored for England after only two minutes. English delirium in the stands! Leonardo Bonucci scored in the second half. Italian joy! England sent up high balls and hoped they would fall for their strikers. They did not. The game ended 1-1.

All this time Grealish sat impatiently on the bench. The fans were desperate to see Jack have a go. But Southgate was in a defensive mood. He only unleashed Jack Grealish in extra time. Sancho and Rashford were subbed on, as a shoot-out loomed. Extra time ended at one each. The whole tournament came down to 10 penalties.

Italy won the toss and took the first spot-kick. Pickford goes to his left. Berardi goes to *his* left! Italy 1-England 0.

Harry Kane steps up for England. He cuts into the bottom left. Donnarumma goes the same way. He's just a fraction too slow, though, and the scores are level at 1-1.

Belotti stutters and sends the ball weakly to the right. Pickford meets it solidly with both palms and pushes it wide! Advantage to England!

McGuire places the ball on the spot. He frowns at the ball and sends it whistling into the top right.

Donnarumma hardly had time to move. England 2-1 up!

Bonucci stabs it into the top left. Pickford gets too little hand on it. Back to level on 2-2. But England still has the advantage.

Rashford loses his balance. He slams it into the left-hand post and it bounces away. England groans! The score stays at 2-2, but now Italy has the advantage!

Bernardeschi drills one down the middle. Pickford misses! Every English fan in the world watches in horror! 3-2 to Italy!

Donnarumma guesses right and puts himself in the way of Sancho's effort. Italy stays one up. Some England fans are hiding behind their couches yet again.

Jorghino skips and rolls the ball to his left. Pickford picks it off! 3-2 to Italy and England is in the last chance saloon.

Saka rockets it to the right. But Donnarumma guesses right! He parries the ball out.

England loses again. The team slumps. Dogs howl. The song stops.

Boris Johnstone tries to think of something funny to say. But nobody in England will be joking for the next little while.

Let me leave it there.

England comes out of Euro 2020 with great honor, but not the cup. The fans all wonder what would have happened if they had seen more of Jack.

## What Next?

Jack Grealish's story continues. We still love to see him in action. Villa fans struggle to see him playing for the Sky Blues, but what can you do? Jack needs to test his strength at the top of the table and against the top European clubs. Villa has some sorting out to do before they get there. Whatever you think about him at Club level, Jack is pure magic for England. No manager is going to play him off the bench the next time. Expect Jack to be on attack for 90 minutes in each game in 2024. Germany hosts the 2024 Euros—we all wonder what they are thinking about Grealish!

Jack will be back!

# Honors

- Aston Villa Youth
    - NextGen Series winner: 2012–13
- Aston Villa
    - EFL Championship play-offs: 2019
    - FA Cup runner-up: 2014–15
    - EFL Cup runner-up: 2019–20
- England U21
    - Toulon Tournament winner: 2016
- England
    - UEFA European Championship runner-up: 2020
- Individual
    - FAI Under-17 Irish International Player of the Year: 2012
    - FAI Under-21 Irish International Player of the Year: 2015
    - Aston Villa Young Player of the Season: 2014–15
    - PFA Team of the Year: 2018–19 (Championship)
    - Aston Villa Player of the Season: 2019–20 (Wikipedia, 2022)

# Some Jack Grealish Trivia

*Why Does Jack Grealish Keep His Socks Rolled Down?*

Jack explains that when he was 15 or 16, the washing machine kept on shrinking his socks. He couldn't pull them up over his muscular calves. He did really well that year—so now he always wears them rolled down for luck!

*Why Does Jack Grealish Wear Such Tiny Shin Pads?*

The team management has never liked Grealish's attitude towards shinguards. Jack thinks they slow him down. As a compromise, Jack wears kid's size 7-8 shin pads.

## *Why Does Jack Grealish Take an Afternoon Nap?*

Two hours of sleep in the middle of the day helps Jack recover. He trains hard in the morning, then rests. He is then ready to go for the afternoon gym work. Sometimes he does an evening session as well.

## *Why Don't the Newspapers Have Stories About Jack Grealish Partying Any More?*

It was the player who almost killed Jack that persuaded him to stop partying, Tom Cleverley. We don't know what he said, but it must have been something like this: "Your mates want you drunk. But I'm also your mate. And I need you sober. You're rubbish when you turn up hungover." Once again Jack had to make a choice. Life is never easy. He cut down on spending time with the mates who could sleep in on Sundays.

## *What Is Jack Grealish's Hairstyle Thing?*

They called them Jack's "Euro curtains." Jack revealed that he had to use Moroccan oil and hair bond to keep his hair in place. Sometimes he has rocked an Alice band or braids. If you are that good you *make* the style. Fans were horrified when he moved on to a side fade and spiky top in February 2022.

### *Why Can Jack Grealish Dribble So Well?*

It comes from balance and technique. He moves the ball with his right foot. But he can jink either way. He slows down and speeds up unexpectedly. Markers try to push him to his left, but he has a technique of getting the ball back on the marker's left side. Jack's body then covers off the defender. At that point, Jack can shoot or pass. It is also the point at which the defender kicks him. That's *what* he does. *How* he does it, nobody knows (Hodson, 2022).

### *Why Does Jack Grealish Roll Up His Shorts?*

Jack explains that he just likes to have bare legs. He thinks it makes him faster. That makes sense-he is faster than anyone else! Nobody wants him to change anything.

### *What Music Does Jack Grealish Listen To?*

Ed Sheeran. Drake. Rihanna. And some oldies: Elvis and Queen!

# Great Grealish Moments

Jack is famous for his mastery of the midfield. He created a shot on goal 98 times in 2021-2022! He also *scores* goals! He has had many moments of greatness!

### *2012: Jack's Under-17 Goals for Ireland*

Young Jack scored three great goals for Ireland's under-17s. One of them was the greatest, but I can't choose!

### *2013: Jack's Gillingham Goal for Notts*

Jack made all the difference to Notts County's season. His goal against Gillingham was his first senior goal. It was an awesome event!

### *2014: Jack's First Outing for Villa Senior Team*

Jack got his first appearance for the Villa senior side. It did not go well for the team, but it showed what Jack could do.

### *2015: Jack's Decision for England*

To be honest, nobody was doing well at the Claret and Blues in 2015. But it was the year Jack decided to play for England!

### *2016: Jack's First Start for England Under-21s*

Jack's first start for England under-21s was immense. He scored two goals against Guinea!

### *2017: Jack's Fantastic Half-a-Season*

Jack scored 5 goals in only half a season for Villa. He was the second-highest goal scorer. Claret and Blue fans thought they were all pretty great.

### *2018: Jack's Cardiff City Missile*

Jack's 20-yard rocket to blast Cardiff City out of the top two was a great moment for him in 2018.

### *2019: Jack's First Match as Captain*

Jack's first match as captain of Villa was great! He scored a goal. Villa beat Derby County 4-0.

### *2020: Jack's Role in Germany's Downfall*

Jack was involved in both goals against Germany in the Euros. That's when he became England's fan-favorite!

## What Did You Think?

First of all, thank you for purchasing this book. We know you could have picked any number of books to read, but you picked this book and for that, we are extremely grateful.

If you enjoyed this book and found some benefit in reading this, we'd love to hear from you and hope that you could take some time to post a review on Amazon. Your feedback and support will help us to know what you like.

You can do this by going to your orders on Amazon and selecting the book and then reviewing it.

Once again from the entire 'My Football Hero' family, thank you!

There are many more books to collect and we're always producing new books. Follow us on Instagram @myfootballhero_ or

Facebook @myfootballhero to hear about new releases.

Please don't forget to review us on Amazon.

Once again.....Thank you!

# References

Aston Villa FC Academy. (2021). *Aston Villa Academy-The Ultimate Guide (Updated 2019)*. PlayerScout. https://playerscout.co.uk/football-academies/english-football-academies/aston-villa-academy/

Callow, J. (2015, May 30). *Arsenal 4-0 Aston Villa: FA Cup Final match report*. The FA.

https://www.thefa.com/news/2015/may/30/the-final-report-300515

Curtis, L. (2021, March 28). *'It wasn't right'-The Notts County story behind England ace Jack Grealish.* Nottingham Post. https://www.nottinghampost.com/sport/football/football-news/jack-grealish-notts-aston-villa-5237616

Fisher, B. (2019, May 14). *Aston Villa beat West Brom on penalties to reach Championship play-off final – as it happened.* The Guardian. https://www.theguardian.com/football/live/2019/may/14/west-brom-v-aston-villa-championship-play-off-semi-final-live

Hodson, T. (2022). *Jack Grealish: Premier League Player Watch.* Coaches' Voice. https://www.coachesvoice.com/cv/jack-grealish-aston-villa/

Lynch, K. (2021, August 6). *Jack Grealish sends emotional message to Aston Villa after Man City move.* Manchester Evening News. https://www.manchestereveningnews.co.uk/sport/football/football-news/man-city-grealish-villa-transfer-21239519

Maltby, M. (2019, May 27). *Aston Villa vs Derby Championship play-off final as it happened*. The Mirror. https://www.mirror.co.uk/sport/football/match-reports/aston-villa-vs-derby-live-16208292

Moxley, N. (2018, May 20). *Villa's Jack Grealish on the innocuous-looking injury that almost killed him*. The Mirror. https://www.mirror.co.uk/sport/football/news/the-surgeon-told-me-jack-12563789

Preece, A. (2021, July 13). *Southgate, Jack Grealish and Toulon as England history repeats itself*. Birmingham Live. https://www.birminghammail.co.uk/sport/football/football-news/jack-grealish-gareth-southgate-england-21045056

ProLyrical. (2022). *We Got Jacky Jack Grealish We Got Kane Lyrics*. Pro Lyrical. https://prolyrical.com/we-got-jacky-jack-grealish-we-got-kane-lyrics/

Regan, M. (2016, September 7). *Jack Grealish: Aston Villa midfielder signs new four-year contract*. BBC. https://www.bbc.com/sport/football/37297039

Skysports. (2021, August 6). *Jack Grealish: Manchester City sign Aston Villa captain for £100m*. Sky Sports. https://www.skysports.com/football/news/11679/12372309/jack-grealish-manchester-city-sign-aston-villa-captain-for-100m

Wikipedia. (2022). *Jack Grealish*. Wikipedia. https://en.wikipedia.org/wiki/Jack_Grealish

Printed in Great Britain
by Amazon